I AM ON INDIGENOUS LAND

written by Katrina M. Phillips   illustrated by Sam Zimmerman

CAPSTONE EDITIONS
a capstone imprint

I hike through the arches on Rainbow Bridge Trail.

I am on Diné land.

I ride my horse through fields of flowers.

I am on Lakota land.

I skate on the ice
when the winter moon glows.

I am on Blackfeet land.

I fish in rivers that lead to the sea.

I am on Nisqually land.

I see fireflies dance on the warm summer breeze.

I am on Shawnee land.

I watch as sea turtles make their way down the beach.

I am on Coast Miwok land.

I explore along paths where wild strawberries grow.

I am on Chickasaw land.

I snowshoe through drifts on a cold winter night.

I am on Ojibwe land.

I hear the waves roar as they rush to the shore.

I am on Taino land.

I bike on trails in
Everglades National Park.

I am on Seminole land.

I smile as my kite soars over the hills.

I am on Tuscarora land.

Whose land are you on?

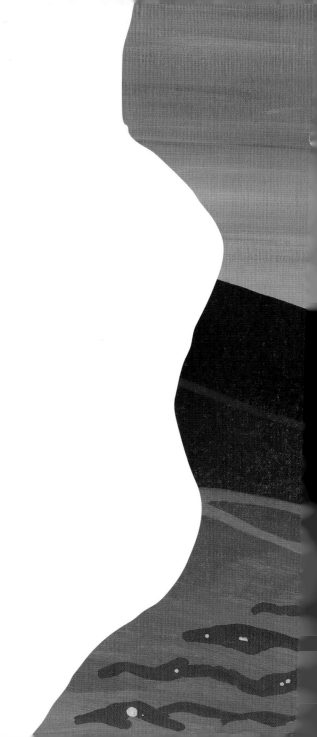

Diné: Rainbow Bridge Trail is part of the Navajo Nation Parks & Recreation in Arizona.

Lakota: Lakota homelands include the Great Plains, where many wildflowers grow.

Blackfeet: The reservation of the Blackfeet Nation is in northern Montana along the Canadian border. It is one of the largest reservations in the United States.

Nisqually: Nisqually activist Billy Frank Jr. was one of the most famous and prominent fishing rights activists of the 1960s and 1970s.

Shawnee: Shawnee people historically lived in the Northeastern Woodlands. Today, there are three Nations of Shawnee: the Absentee Shawnee, the Eastern Shawnee Tribe, and the Shawnee Tribe.

Coast Miwok: Coast Miwok people have a long history in what's now California. Historically, the ocean provided almost everything they needed.

Chickasaw: Strawberries are among the native plants that are culturally important to the Chickasaw people. Traditional Chickasaw summer houses are small huts that provide protection from sun and rain.

Ojibwe: Ojibwe people aren't the only Indigenous people who traditionally used snowshoes, but they're well-known for these special shoes that make it possible to walk on top of deep snow.

Taíno: Historically, the Taíno lived in the area we now know as the Caribbean. They grew crops like sweet potatoes, maize, and beans.

Seminole: The Everglades in Florida have long been important to Seminole people. Today, there are five biking trails through the Everglades.

Ho-Chunk: The Ho-Chunk are one of eleven federally recognized Nations in Wisconsin, and the Wisconsin Dells are famous for their water parks and tourism.

Tuscarora: The Tuscarora Reservation is in Niagara County, New York. They are one of the six Nations of the Haudenosaunee Confederacy.

Learn More About
Indigenous Lands

Indigenous people have called this land home for thousands of years. Indigenous means native, or those who first belonged. Some Indigenous people farmed or fished to feed their families. Others traveled or migrated as seasons changed, or they followed the animals they hunted. But when Europeans began arriving on Indigenous lands, they colonized much of the continent, which means they took the land for themselves. More and more non-Indigenous people moved to North America, and they forced Indigenous people from their homelands again and again and again.

The numbers on this map indicate the regional homelands of 12 Indigenous Nations. Today, there are Indigenous Nations all across North America and millions of Indigenous peoples around the world. It is important for all of us to understand that the lands where we live, play, and go to school, the roads that we drive on, and the hills, valleys, rivers, lakes, beaches, and bluffs that we love, were first home to Indigenous people. Caring for the land and knowing whose lands you live on—whether Ojibwe, Nisqually, Seminole, or any of hundreds of other Indigenous Nations—are some of the ways we can honor and respect the people who first belonged.

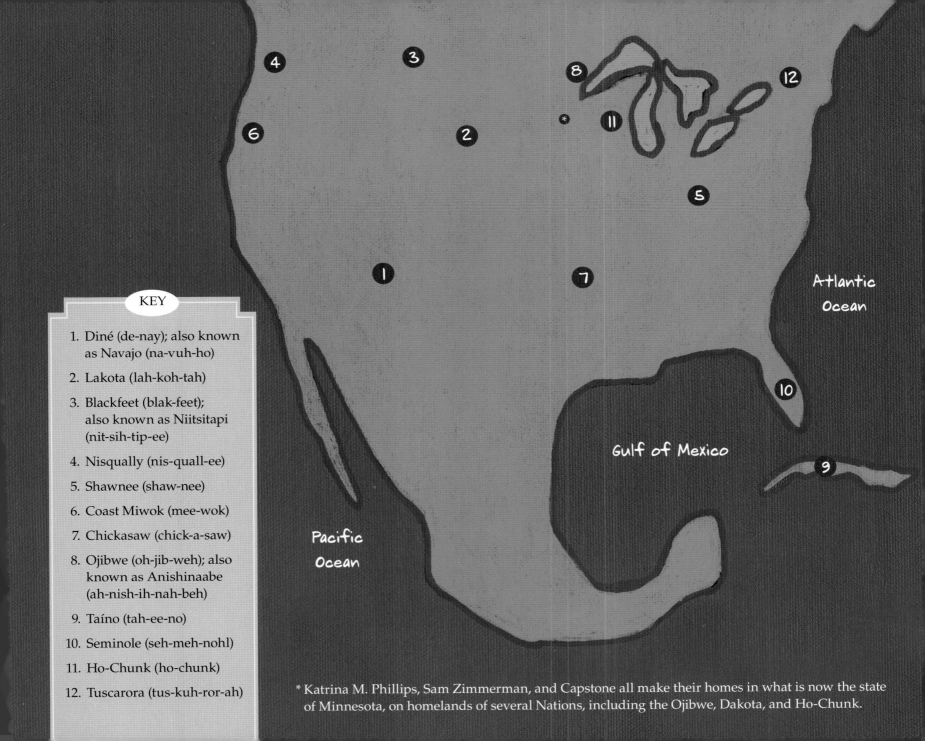

KEY

1. Diné (de-nay); also known as Navajo (na-vuh-ho)

2. Lakota (lah-koh-tah)

3. Blackfeet (blak-feet); also known as Niitsitapi (nit-sih-tip-ee)

4. Nisqually (nis-quall-ee)

5. Shawnee (shaw-nee)

6. Coast Miwok (mee-wok)

7. Chickasaw (chick-a-saw)

8. Ojibwe (oh-jib-weh); also known as Anishinaabe (ah-nish-ih-nah-beh)

9. Taíno (tah-ee-no)

10. Seminole (seh-meh-nohl)

11. Ho-Chunk (ho-chunk)

12. Tuscarora (tus-kuh-ror-ah)

Atlantic Ocean

Gulf of Mexico

Pacific Ocean

* Katrina M. Phillips, Sam Zimmerman, and Capstone all make their homes in what is now the state of Minnesota, on homelands of several Nations, including the Ojibwe, Dakota, and Ho-Chunk.

About the Author

Dr. Katrina M. Phillips is a citizen of the Red Cliff Band of Lake Superior Ojibwe. She has a BA and PhD in History from the University of Minnesota and is a history professor at Macalester College in St. Paul. In addition to her scholarly work, she's written a number of children's books that focus on Native peoples and Native histories, including *Indigenous Peoples' Day*; *Indigenous Peoples: Women Who Made a Difference* (Super SHEroes of History); and *The Untold Story of Mary Golda Ross: Pioneering Space Engineer* (First But Forgotten).

About the Illustrator

Sam Zimmerman (Zhaawanoogiizhik), a Grand Portage Band of Ojibwe direct descendant, returned home to Minnesota and Grand Portage on the north shore of Lake Superior after a career in education on the east coast. He rededicated himself to painting as a means of exploring his Ojibwe heritage, his experiences in nature, and Anishinaabe traditions of storytelling. Sam focuses on themes of environmental stewardship and conservation through his studio and public art commissions, which include pieces for the Chik-Wauk Museum and Nature Center, Voyageurs National Park, and the Minnesota communities of Duluth and Grand Marais. Sam has been the recipient of grant awards from the Minnesota State Arts Board, Arrowhead Regional Arts Council, and Duluth Superior Community Foundation. He has also worked to help preserve the Ojibwemowin language by creating bilingual books, including *Following My Spirit Home*. Sam's work is displayed in galleries, private collections, and @CraneSuperior on Instagram.

Published by Capstone Editions, an imprint of Capstone
1710 Roe Crest Drive
North Mankato, Minnesota 56003
capstonepub.com

Text copyright © 2025 by Capstone.
Illustrations copyright © 2025 by Sam Zimmerman.

Library of Congress Cataloging-in-Publication Data is available on the Library of Congress website.
ISBN 9781684363087 (hardcover)
ISBN 9781684363094 (ebook PDF)

Designers: Nathan Gassman and Sarah Bennett

Printed and bound in China. PO 6193

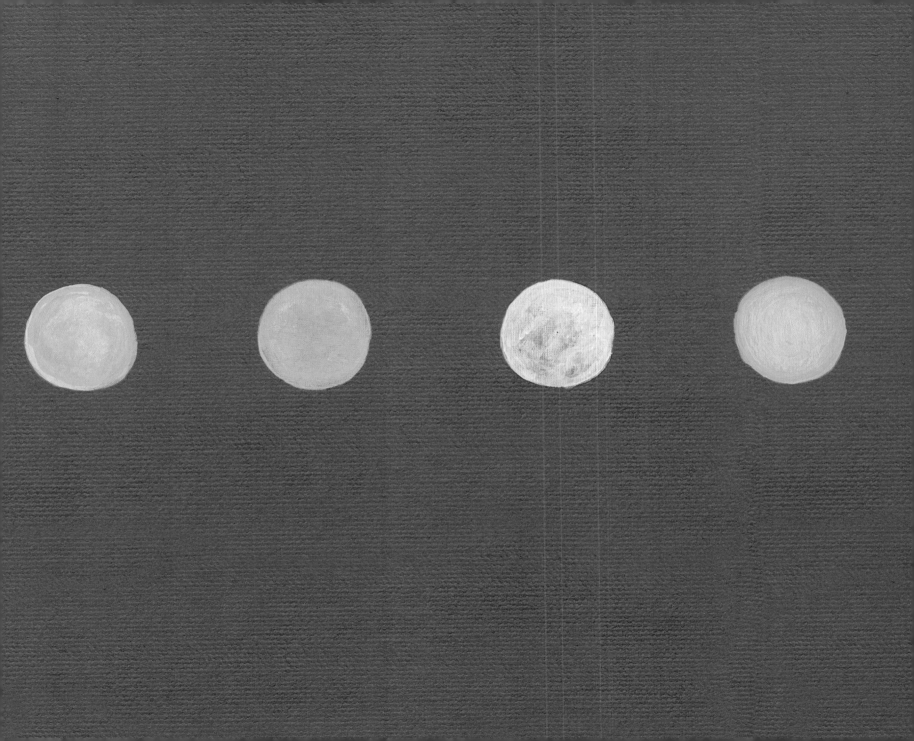

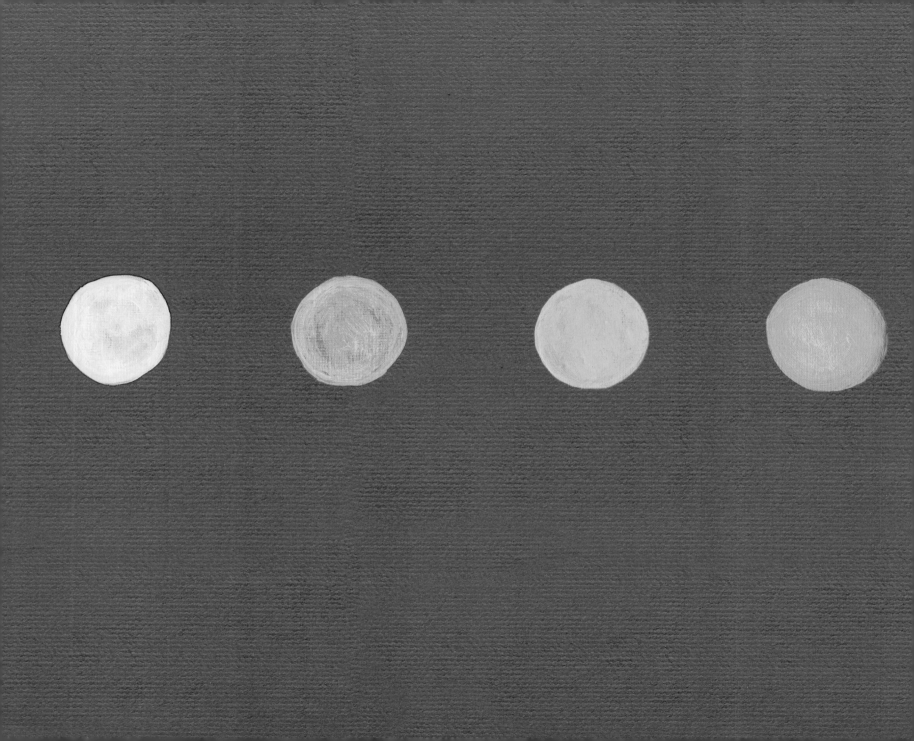